Ultimate Beginner Tech Start Series
Musicians And Computi...

By David S. Mash

£7.00

WARNER BROS. PUBLICATIONS - THE GLOBAL LEADER IN PRINT
USA: 15800 NW 48th Avenue, Miami, FL 33014

8/98

WARNER/CHAPPELL MUSIC

CANADA: 85 SCARSDALE ROAD, SUITE 101
DON MILLS, ONTARIO, M3B 2R2
SCANDINAVIA: P.O. BOX 533, VENDEVAGEN 85 B
S-182 15, DANDERYD, SWEDEN
AUSTRALIA: P.O. BOX 353
3 TALAVERA ROAD, NORTH RYDE N.S.W. 2113

NUOVA CARISCH

ITALY: VIA CAMPANIA, 12
20098 S. GIULIANO MILANESE (MI)
ZONA INDUSTRIALE SESTO ULTERIANO
SPAIN: MAGALLANES, 25
28015 MADRID
FRANCE: 25 RUE DE HAUTEVILLE, 75010 PARIS

IMP

INTERNATIONAL MUSIC PUBLICATIONS LIMITED

ENGLAND: SOUTHEND ROAD,
WOODFORD GREEN, ESSEX IG8 8HN
GERMANY: MARSTALLSTR. 8, D-80539 MUNCHEN
DENMARK: DANMUSIK, VOGNMAGERGADE 7
DK 1120 KOBENHAVNK

Editor: Debbie Cavalier
Cover Design: Debbie Johns Lipton
Cover Illustration: Jorge Paredes
Layout: Debbie Johns Lipton, Jorge Paredes
Character Illustration: Ken Rehm

Dedication & Thanks

This book is dedicated to my friends and colleagues at Berklee College of Music. Special thanks to Erica Mash, Debbie Cavalier, David Lustig, Lee Whitmore, Steve Lipson, Joan Wood, and Jennifer Smith.

Contents

Introduction

So you have read in all the magazines and heard from all your friends just what a great asset a computer can be to you as a musician, and you've finally decided to take the plunge. But how do you get started? This book is an introduction to computers specifically aimed at meeting the unique needs of musicians. It is a primer for using computers in your musical work and daily life, and a guide to the kinds of systems and software available to make you as productive as possible.

We'll examine what a computer is and how it works; how you can use it to make music; how to connect it to other devices using the MIDI (Musical Instrument Digital Interface) system; we'll begin to see the computer as part of your musical instrument and learn practice techniques that will help you master it as an instrument; and how you can use it to manage your music career—keeping track of gigs, musicians' contact information, expenses and income, and promoting your work!

If you don't have a computer, this book will help you in making your purchasing decisions—if you already own a computer, you'll learn how to configure it for making music. We'll demystify all the buzz words, cryptic acronyms, collections of initials; translate all the geek-speak, explain what it all means, and relate it to your needs as a musician. We'll explore a variety of applications that will forever change how you view the personal computer.

So let's get started and find out what makes a personal computer tick!

Chapter One

What Is A Computer?

Today there are many types of personal computers—they come in all sizes, shapes, colors, brands, models, and with every conceivable combination of letters and numbers as acronyms describing their various functions and configurations. It seems like a totally incomprehensible world at first, but actually, all computers are comprised of a few simple basic components. Once we understand how these components work together to make a complete system called a computer, it will all become quite clear and manageable.

While certainly an oversimplification, we can look at the computer as basically consisting of four components:

- a processor, which is the device that does the actual computing;
- memory, which is the space in which the computing takes place;
- input/output devices, which are how you enter and view information; and
- storage, which is where the information is semi-permanently retained.

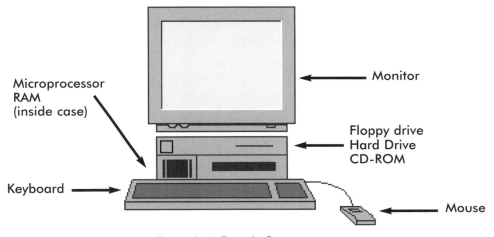

Figure 1: A Generic Computer

Let's examine each of these components in a little greater depth.

Processor

Computers basically do one task—they process numbers. So we might describe the microprocessor, then, as being the brain of the computer. And in spite of how much intelligence we generally ascribe to the computer, it basically sees the world of information in only one of two states: everything is either on or off—ones or zeroes. Each of these zeroes and ones is called a bit and constitutes one digit or letter in a digital word, called a byte. Everything a computer does is a function of bits and bytes of information, numbers which are processed by the microprocessor. In describing the amount of information a computer processes we usually speak in multiples of bits and bytes, and use the Latin prefixes kilo for thousands (kilobytes), mega for millions (megabytes), and giga for thousands of millions (gigabytes).

Today, personal computers generally use one of two types of microprocessors to perform their computing tasks: either a complex instruction set computer (CISC) chip (i.e., 80486, 80586, Pentium, etc.) usually made by Intel or one of its licensees, or a reduced instruction set computer (RISC) chip (i.e., PPC 603, 604, 750, etc.) usually made by IBM, Motorola, or one of their licensees. Intel chips are used in computers which are designed to run Microsoft's Windows operating system (often called "Wintel machines"), while the RISC or PowerPC chips are used in computers which run Apple Computer's Macintosh operating system (MacOS).

Microprocessors are rated by the number of bits they can process at a time and by how fast their clocks run, which determines the number of instructions that can be executed per second. So a typical contemporary microprocessor might be classified as a 32 bit processor running at 200 megahertz (MHz) or 200 million instructions per second. In simplest terms the more bits that can be processed per cycle, and the more cycles that occur per second, the more powerful a computer. There are many other elements that affect the speed of operation as well, but none that have as big an impact on the raw computing power as the speed of the microprocessor.

There is always a trade-off between power and cost, and typically the speed and power of computers doubles every eighteen months. (There is a folklore rule called "Moore's Law": Gordon Moore, Co-Founder of Intel, once noted that Intel's chips had basically doubled in speed and power each year, and he expected that pace would continue for the foreseeable future. He later revised that timetable to every two years, and today most people misquote Moore's Law as saying that the speed of chips will continue to double every 18 months.) Since speed increases are desirable in computers, resale values of computers are inversely proportionate to Moore's Law—they seem to half in value every eighteen months or so. Therefore, you might want to buy the most powerful processor you can, as not only will it enhance the kind of work you'll be able to do, but it will protect your investment for a little longer.

Memory

Computer memory that can be written to and read from at will is called Random Access Memory (RAM). RAM is the space in which the computer performs its actions—instructions from the operating system and application software are read into this space and held for a short period of time, and the information being processed is also held in this space as well. The more RAM, the more instructions and data can be worked upon at once, therefore increasing the perceived speed and functionality of the computer. However, RAM is not permanent; when the power is switched off, or an error occurs, the information previously held in RAM is lost, necessitating some more permanent form of storage space.

Information held in RAM may be accessed by the microprocessor faster than from any type of permanent storage media, so by having ample amounts of RAM available, the computer will have to access the storage medium less frequently, thereby speeding up your work. Also, the more RAM available, the bigger the files (like digital audio or video) you will be able to process. Finally, more RAM allows more application software to be open at any given time, allowing you to work in a more efficient manner.

Don't be fooled by schemes which use Virtual Memory in place of actual RAM, as these use an area of storage media such as a hard drive as temporary memory space. While these allow you to open more applications at once, they don't speed your work because access from the storage media is always slower than real RAM. Also if you are using your computer for digital audio or video, the software will try to read in the file from disk and hold it in RAM while you work on it or play it back. If you are using Virtual Memory instead of RAM, the processor will read the file from disk and store it back to disk, thereby slowing all the processes to a crawl, or perhaps failing entirely. (Perhaps you have heard the word "crash"?)

Storage

There are many types of storage media available for computers today:

- Floppy Disks
- Hard Disks
- Removable Media
- CD-ROM
- Magnetic Tape

Each of these storage devices has a specific value depending on cost, speed of access, long-term reliability, and size of installed base.

Floppy disks are generally widely available; almost every computer has one, so you can be reasonably assured that if you try to exchange data with someone else via floppy disk, they will most likely have a means of reading the data. Floppy disks today come in a variety of formats, the most popular being the 3.5" diskette which comes in single-sided, double-sided, and high-density formats holding between 400 kilobytes (thousands of bytes) and 1.4 megabytes (millions of bytes) of information. Floppy disks are cheap, reasonably reliable, have an enormous installed base as almost all computers now routinely include them, but are relatively small in storage capacity and slow in data access time. Figure 2 shows a floppy disk and drive.

Figure 2: A Floppy Disk And Drive

Hard disks are very widely used both as internal devices (that is, included inside the computer case) and as external add-on drives. Hard drives come in a wide variety of storage capacity from 20 megabytes to multiple gigabytes (a gigabyte is a thousand megabytes!), and are some of the fastest storage devices available. Today, hard disks are fast, big, and ubiquitous, although since the data is stored on platters which cannot be removed from the computer or the external drive, sharing data between computers is a little less convenient, requiring you to physically detach, move and reattach the drive from one machine to another. Figure 3 shows an external hard disk drive.

Figure 3: An External Hard Disk Drive

This difficulty in sharing data between computers is somewhat overcome by a type of storage device that uses removable media. These devices come in two parts: the drive and the media. Media is inserted into the drive (as with a floppy disk), written to and read from, then removed for off-line storage. Removable media is good for backing up information (copying information from a fixed hard drive and storing it off-line on removable media, thereby having a back-up copy in case anything happens to the original information). The type of media used determines the quantity of data that may be stored, the speed of access, the reliability of the storage, and the overall storage cost. Also some formats are more commonly used than others making it more or less easy to share your data. Some commonly used removable media devices are:

- Zip Drives: inexpensive cartridges that hold 100 megabytes of data. Zip drives are fairly reliable and have a very large installed base.
- Magneto-Optical Disks: slightly more expensive disks that hold between 128 megabytes to 4 gigabytes of data. MO disks are extremely reliable with a very long shelf life, but are used less extensively, as the wide variety of different formats are incompatible with one another.
- Syquest Cartridges: fairly expensive cartridges that provide storage capacities between 44 megabytes and 1.5 gigabytes. Syquest cartridges are fairly reliable but are used less extensively because the various formats are incompatible with one another.
- JAZ Drives: fairly expensive cartridges that hold either one or two gigabytes of data. JAZ drives are very reliable and widely used today by media professionals (like musicians). And almost 2 CDs worth of music can be stored on a single 1-gigabyte cartridge.

Figure 4: Removable Media Devices

CD-ROM drives are read-only storage media good for music and multimedia titles. A lot of popular software is now distributed via CD-ROM and most computers include them in their base configurations. While widely available and inexpensive, CD-ROM drives have fairly slow access times. Recordable CD writers (CD-R drives) are becoming more common these days for musicians; they cost less than $500, and allow you to write your own CDs with either data or sound onto blank media which is now available at extremely low cost (often less than DAT or videotape). These CD-R drives allow you to create music CDs that may be played back on any standard audio CD player, and used to mass produce your own recordings.

Figure 5: A CD-ROM Drive

Magnetic tape is used mostly for backup, as its slow access time makes it unusable for real-time data storage and retrieval. However, a single 4 mm tape cartridge (the size and shape of a standard audio DAT but specially designed for data use) can store many gigabytes of information, making it the most inexpensive way to back up data for off-line storage. Figure 6 shows a 4 mm DAT backup device.

Figure 6: A DAT Backup Drive

Since we will be using our computers for music, we should be aware that digital audio files are quite large—it takes 10 megabytes to store each minute of stereo sound at CD quality. Therefore, having as much RAM and as large a storage device as possible is very desirable, as are removable media drives such as the JAZ drive discussed above. So the old adage that you can never be too rich or too thin may be thusly applied to computers: You can never have too much RAM or too big of a hard drive!

Input/Output Devices

Input and output devices allow you to enter, manipulate, view, print, and communicate your data. Let's first look at the variety of devices available today for inputting and manipulating information. The most common of these are the alpha-numeric keyboard, mouse, trackball, trackpad, joystick, and graphic tablet. The alpha-numeric keyboard is used for entering text and numbers into programs, as well as for basic keyboard commands for various computer and software operations.

The mouse, first popularized by the Macintosh computer and now ubiquitous on all forms of personal computers, is a very powerful and useful device for pointing and clicking at items on a screen. The mouse is rolled around the physical desktop while the cursor moves in an analogous manner on the screen (a virtual desktop). The button (or buttons) on a mouse can then be pressed to simulate the pressing of an on-screen button. Figure 7 shows a typical alpha-numeric keyboard and mouse.

Figure 7: Alpha-Numeric Keyboard And Mouse

Trackballs and trackpads are substitute point-and-click devices for the mouse, and are useful in situations where desk space is at a premium (like in a recording studio), because the devices themselves remain stationary and only the ball (in the case of trackballs) or finger (in the case of trackpads) are moved. Figure 8 shows trackball and trackpad devices.

Figure 8: Trackpad And Trackball Devices

Joysticks are commonly used for input to games, and graphics tablets are used with special pens by artists for drawing onto the computer screen. While both of these devices (as well as more esoteric input devices such as glove controllers, head tracking devices, and others) may have useful applications to music making, we will not go into them in greater detail at this time.

Monitors

Inputting data into the computer is not of much value if you cannot see the results of this input, so let's focus a bit on output devices. The most common output device for a computer is the monitor display. Monitors come in a wide variety of physical sizes and shapes, and support a number of different image resolutions in monochrome (black and white), gray-scale, and color formats. Monitors are usually measured in inches, diagonally across the screen much as are televisions. Common sizes range between thirteen and twenty-one inches.

Screen resolution is measured in the number of pixels that can be displayed horizontally by vertically. (Pixels are small dots, so-named because they are small elements which comprise the total picture—PIctureXELement = pixel.) Common screen resolutions are 640x480 (VGA), 800x600 (SVGA), 640x870 (Portrait), 832x624, 1024x768, and 1152x870. Some monitors are called multi-sync monitors and are capable of displaying a variety of different resolutions on their single physical screen size.

The number of colors or shades of gray that can be displayed is usually determined by the monitor, the display card or hardware which drives the monitor, and the amount of memory allocated to video imaging (VRAM). Although music notation requires only monochrome display, many musicians prefer color monitors because modern software makes good use of the color to distinguish amongst tracks, instruments, and MIDI channels in sequencing and digital audio editing programs.

The bigger the monitor, the more information that can be seen at once, so once again you may use the principle that bigger is better, until you run out of physical desktop space. While the vast majority of monitors on the market today use cathode ray tubes for creating the image (hence the common acronym CRT for monitor), an increasing number of monitors are now available which use flat Liquid Crystal Displays (LCDs) much like those used in portable or laptop computers. These allow for large viewable areas with bright colors in very small packages, and while more expensive at this time, the prices are dropping as more units are manufactured and sold.

If you will use your computer for creating music for visual images, you may want to use two monitors, one for displaying your music software and data, the other for displaying video or pictures. We'll return to this later when we discuss specific applications.

Printers

If you will be doing a lot of music notation with your computer, you may want to consider a high quality printer for outputting your scores and parts. There are a number of different kinds of printers, but the two most common are ink-jet and laser printers. Ink jets work by spraying ink through tiny holes to create the image in either black and white, gray-scale, or full color. Laser printers use a laser ray to fuse ink from a toner cartridge onto the paper. Like monitors, printers come in a number of resolutions, measured in the number of dots per inch placed on the paper. Inexpensive printers commonly provide 300x300 dots per inch (dpi) or 600x600 dpi. More costly professional printers provide 1200, 1800, or 2400 dpi output.

Many music notation packages are capable of using a technology developed by Adobe, Inc. called PostScript. This technology allows for the printer to create the graphic notation image by creating shapes derived from mathematical formulae rather than collections of small dots. This allows for very high quality output, rivaling traditional music engraving. The notation programs include special typefaces (called fonts) in the PostScript format, and PostScript-compatible laser printers take advantage of these for providing very high quality print output. This is especially noticeable on expression markings such as slurs, articulations, and crescendi and decrescendi.

Sound

Sound (audio) is another important output format for musicians. Today, most computers have some form of sound output capability either as a sound card in an expansion slot, or built directly into the computer's main logic board. The computer (or sometimes the monitor) may have built-in speakers or some form of output jack for connecting the computer to an external sound system. Many computers also have sound-input capability for recording sound into the computer. There are also add-on cards for most computers which provide for multi-channel audio recording and playback, or provide digital inputs and outputs so that the computer may be integrated into a professional recording environment. We will return to this later in Chapter Two: Configuring Your Computer For Music.

In addition to keyboards, mice, monitors, and printers, computers may also provide input/output connectivity for Local Area Networks (LANs) or modems for connections to the Internet. Sometimes these capabilities are built-in, other times connection ports are provided either inside the computer as expansion slots or outside of the computer case as expansion ports. Common ports included on many computers are serial or parallel ports for connecting input and output devices; SCSI (Small Computer System Interface, pronounced as "scuzzy"), used for connecting storage devices; slots for connecting PC card devices; internal expansion slots (usually using the Peripheral Connect Interface [PCI] standard).

Form Factor

Another decision factor in choosing a computer is whether to buy a desktop, tower, or portable machine. Figures 9, 10, and 11 show the three most common form factors for computers today:

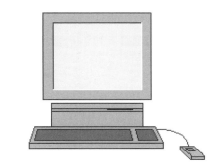

Figure 9: Desktop Computer Form Factor

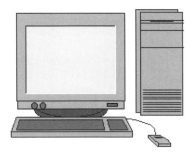

Figure 10: Tower Computer Form Factor

Figure 11: Portable Computer Form Factor

Desktop computers are good for musicians who will use their machines for most basic musical applications, who want to allow for some expandability in the future, but who do not need to travel with the computer. Tower machines are better for those who plan to use more advanced applications as these form factors allow for more internal storage devices and usually provide a greater number of expansion slots for adding cards for digital audio and video processing. Portable computers are good for traveling musicians who use their computers for staying in touch with e-mail while traveling or who need MIDI sequence playback on stage. For more rigorous use on stage, many musicians have desktop computers converted to rack-mount units for use in shock-mount road cases to protect their machines during travel and for better integration into more complex MIDI stage setups.

As I said when we began this exploration of the components that make up a computer, this is an incredible simplification of the topic. There are other aspects to a computer's architecture than those we have just examined, and some of these have a major impact on how the computer operates. To close this section on the hardware aspect of computers, let's take a quick look at two other items that are often included in advertisements that provide specifications about the computer and its configuration.

The speed of the bus—the data connection which interconnects all of the components we described above—is one factor which affects how fast a computer operates. How fast the processor is able to communicate with the memory, storage, and input/output devices depends on the speed of the bus, and this is again usually referred to in megahertz (MHz). Typical bus speeds are upwards of 50 or 60 MHz, and of course—the faster the better.

A second oft-referred to specification is called "level-2 cache." A cache is a small amount of memory usually set aside for storing frequently-used instructions from the software. Many chips have a small (32 or 64 kilobytes) amount of cache built right into the microprocessor. Level 2 cache (or L2 Cache) is memory which is directly connected to the processor chip, via a very high speed bus. The bigger this cache, the less frequently the computer has to go to storage or even to RAM to get the instructions it uses most often, thus providing even more processing speed. A fairly new development in this concept is called backside cache, which is off-chip cache connected by a bus half the speed of the clock, which can be quite large—a megabyte or even larger—yielding incredible speeds for processing information!

In spite of the time we have just spent examining the various hardware components, computers are nothing more than interestingly designed furniture. It is the software that tells them what and how to do the various things that make them become useful tools. So let's now turn our attention away from the physical components that make up a computer and explore the various software that makes them work for us.

Software

We can divide software into two basic categories: operating system software and application software. Operating system software (OS) tells the computer how to do its most basic tasks, and controls the overall look and feel of the computer environment. Application software is the individual productivity tool we use for performing specific tasks such as word processing, music notation, digital audio recording and editing, running our daily calendars, and doing our taxes. Again, this is a slight over-simplification as there are many subtle categories of software which fall someplace in between these two major poles—utilities, desk accessories, control panels, etc. We will discuss some of these as we progress through Chapters Three through Six.

Operating System

There are basically two standards in the personal computer world today: those that use Pentium microprocessors from Intel or its licensee manufacturers and run the Windows operating system from Microsoft; and those that use the PowerPC microprocessor from Motorola and IBM and run the Macintosh Operating System from Apple Computer. There are a number of other operating systems available today with very small market shares in the personal computer market such as NeXtStep, IBM's OS/2, and BeOS, but for the scope of a book this short, we'll focus on the two major players for personal computers used by musicians: Windows and MacOS. While it is true that Windows far overshadows the MacOS in business applications, the MacOS is still by far the dominant system in use worldwide by professional musicians.

If you do not already own a computer, selecting the software which operates your computer is one of the most important decisions you will make when determining which computer hardware you will buy. Both Windows and the MacOS are graphical-based operating systems, but MacOS is more closely integrated with the hardware than is Windows (due to the large number of generic "Wintel" computer makers and the variety of hardware configurations available compared to the single standard set by Apple Computer for the integration of Macintosh hardware and software). This gives the Macintosh a small edge in ease of connectivity and configuration of peripheral devices. Most of the application software we will explore throughout this book, however, is available for both Windows and Macintosh operating systems.

Figures 12 and 13 show the Windows95 and Macintosh desktops, respectively.

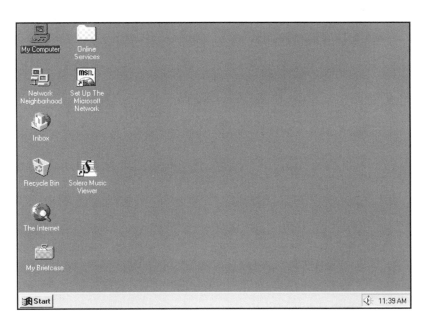

Figure 12: The Windows95 Desktop

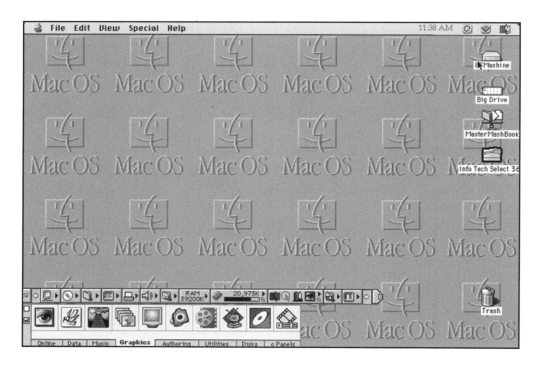

Figure 13: The Macintosh Desktop

Application Software

Regardless of which computer platform you use, application software packages provide the basic tools you use to accomplish specific tasks such as MIDI sequencing, music notation, audio recording and editing, word processing, graphics, tracking your contacts, keeping your schedule and budget, and communicating with others via electronic mail, the World Wide Web, and the Internet. Most application software is now available for both Windows and Macintosh computers; however, there are a few packages that are unique to one or the other system usually due to perceived market needs or integration needs between hardware and software.

Now that we have a basic understanding of what a computer is and how it works, let's delve a little deeper into exactly how we set up a computer for making music, and how it can be integrated into a more expanded music system, integrating both audio and MIDI devices with our computer hardware and software.

Chapter Two
Configuring Your Computer For Music

Whether using a computer on a desktop, in a studio, or on the road with a laptop, computers have become indispensable devices for the musician. Whether you are studying music, working professionally, or hoping to do either, a computer will make many tasks more simple, less filled with drudgery, and can help you do things not otherwise possible. In this chapter we will discuss how to configure a computer for music making, including how to connect your computer to a sound system, how to integrate your computer into a MIDI system, and the types of hardware and software configurations that will optimize your computer's musical performance.

As we mentioned in Chapter One, music makes strong demands on a computer system. Digital audio files are large—10 megabytes for each stereo minute of CD quality sound—and that places a demand on storage, memory, and processor speed. If you are recording audio, you will need hardware that can convert analog audio into digital files; RAM for temporary storage while you listen to or edit the file; plenty of storage for the files themselves; and room for storing edits in progress. Your processor and hardware bus will need to be powerful enough to handle all the input and output tasks at once!

If you plan to use music notation, you will be displaying large graphic files and will need both processor speed as well as video memory in order to display the graphics in synchronicity with music playback. If you intend to do MIDI work, you will need a way to connect to MIDI synthesizers, and you may also need to synchronize your MIDI data with digital audio and even video. And trust me, even if you don't think you will want to do these things right away, as soon as you start using your computer for music making, you will see just how valuable a tool a computer can be, and you will want to start doing more and more complex work with your machine.

So, the first recommendation we have for configuring your computer is to get the biggest, fastest hard drive you can afford. If possible, get a removable drive as well. Spend as much as you can to get plenty of RAM. And if you are buying a new machine—or if your existing computer has the capability for upgrading its microprocessor—get the fastest processor available. By building the most powerful machine you can afford, you can hedge against obsolescence, and blaze through your work with enjoyment rather than frustration. I have two computers: one for my studio—fully integrated with a large MIDI system, digital audio and video systems—and a laptop for use on the road.

Both of my machines are configured with 80 megabytes of RAM and have 200 megahertz processors. My studio machine has two internal hard drives (one is 2 gigabytes, the other is 4 gigabytes), an external 6 gigabyte hard drive, a 1 gigabyte JAZ removable drive, a 230 megabyte Magneto-Optical drive, a 24x CD-ROM drive and a 4x Read and Write CD-R drive. My laptop has a 2 gigabyte internal hard drive, a 12x CD-ROM, and a 230 megabyte Magneto-Optical drive (which makes moving files between studio and the road a cinch). And by the time this goes to print both machines will be dwarfed by newer models with faster processors, more available RAM and bigger hard drives!

You will want to get as large a multi-sync monitor as your working space and budget will allow. I recommend at least a 15" monitor but optimally a 17" or larger will help you see more information on screen and work faster and smarter. If you will be doing music for video or animations, you will probably want to add a second video card to your computer (perhaps one that provides the capabilities of capturing and digitizing video) to drive a second monitor. If so, the second monitor may be of any size as long as it is capable of displaying 640x480 (VGA) resolution.

Once you have configured your hardware with plenty of RAM, hard disk space, and a fast processor, it's time to start connecting your hardware to music systems. Let's start with the audio connections.

Connecting Your Computer To
An External Sound System

If your computer has an internal sound card or, like all Macintosh computers, has sound integrated on the main logic board, you will have some form of speaker jack available on the back of the computer. Generally these are small stereo jacks that defeat any internal speaker or speakers when a plug is inserted. These jacks are usually optimized for line level output, and will either require a stereo amplifier or amplified speakers. Many external speakers designed for computers are self-amplified and are optimized for a computers' digital audio. Some of these are configured as two small stereo speakers with a sub-woofer for producing the bass frequencies. Many of these are also specially shielded to avoid magnetic interference with the computer monitor. As a musician, sound quality is of utmost importance, so you should connect your computer to the highest quality sound system available.

In order to do this, we must understand the basic hardware of connecting audio: jacks, plugs, cables, and adapters. Jacks are receptacle connectors, into which plugs are inserted. Jacks and plugs are often referred to as "female" and "male" connectors respectively. Cables are the wires which carry signals, and usually have either plugs or jacks at each end. Adapters are devices which allow jacks and plugs of differing configurations to be used together without the need for creating specialized cables for every situation. Adapters usually have a jack on one end and a plug of a different size and shape at the other. In general, most devices have jacks on their panels for both input and output, and cables with plugs at both ends are used to make connections between devices.

Most computers provide 1/8 inch connectors called mini phone jacks for audio connections. Computers with stereo capability use three conductor jacks (sometimes called TRS jacks—for tip, ring, and sleeve—referring to the three conductor elements), monophonic machines use two conductor jacks. If the sound system to which you wish to connect is stereo and uses standard phono jacks (often called RCA jacks), you will need to purchase adapters for making the connections. Figure 14 shows the most common types of plugs and adapter plugs for connecting a computer's sound output to various speakers or stereo sound systems.

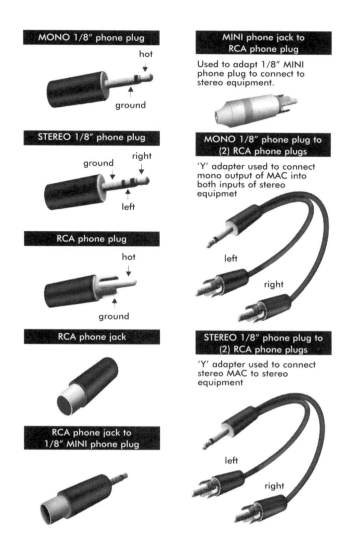

Figure 14: Common Audio Jacks, Plugs, And Adapters

Figure 15 shows the most common ways to connect your computer to either powered speakers or a stereo system. Most powered speakers use 1/8 inch stereo mini plugs for connections, while stereo systems usually provide RCA phono jacks for input and outputs.

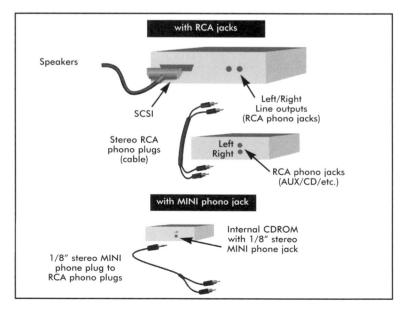

Figure 15: Connecting Your Computer To A Sound System

Audio From CD

You may already have a CD-ROM drive attached to your computer which you can use to play audio compact discs as well. CD audio is the industry standard for high quality digital sound. By connecting the audio outputs from your CD-ROM drive to a stereo speaker system you can easily use CD audio for a variety of musical applications, including music-minus-one style play-along. Some internal CD-ROM drives have their audio connections made directly through the computer's sound output jack (see above), but external drives will need a separate audio connection. Figure 16 shows the most common audio connections for CD-ROM drives.

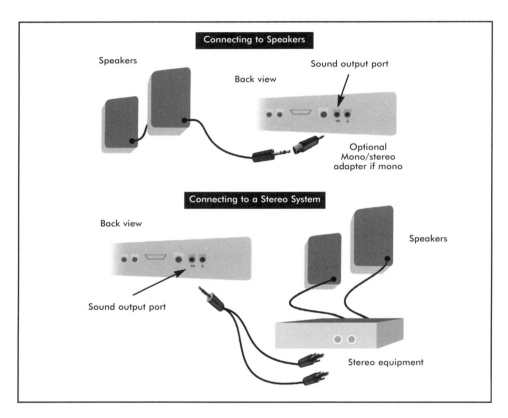

Figure 16: Connecting Your CD-ROM Drive's Audio

Sound Input Devices

If your computer does not have a built-in audio input jack, you may want to add an audio digitizer using either an internal expansion card, or a serial port or PC card slot for connecting an external or removable device. High quality audio input devices are available for all personal computers that add the capability of recording and playing back digital audio with compact disc fidelity. Popular choices available for both Macintosh as well as Windows machines are the Audiomedia III card from Digidesign and the Korg 1212 I/O card. Both of these cards offers stereo recording and playback capability with CD quality sound, with both analog and digital inputs and outputs. The Korg card also adds 8 channels of digital audio input and output using the ADAT optical format.

These cards (and other fine products like them) allow you to do professional quality audio recording and playback with both analog and digital inputs and outputs for less than a thousand dollars. Connections vary by card manufacturer (the Digidesign card uses RCA phono jacks, while the Korg uses 1/4 inch TRS stereo jacks for analog audio, RCA phono jacks for stereo digital audio, and ADAT optical connectors for multi-channel digital audio), so you should see the card's owner's manual for appropriate connection directions.

Figure 17: The Korg 1212 I/O Card

MIDI

MIDI is an acronym for the Musical Instrument Digital Interface. MIDI is a protocol that allows computers, synthesizers, and other musical instruments and devices to communicate with one another. By connecting your computer to a MIDI synthesizer, you can take advantage of all of the high quality sounds stored in the instrument's memory. MIDI data consists of when a note is played, which note is played, how loud the note is played, and when the note is stopped. Every note played (and eventually stopped) therefore consists of six bytes of information:

    1) That a note is to be played;
    2) Which note is to be played;
    3) The velocity value for the note (which most often translates into volume);
    4) That a note is to be ended;
    5) Which note is to end (because there may be many notes playing at once); and
    6) How quickly the note is to be stopped (which might affect the release time of the sound).

In addition to this information, MIDI also carries signals which control the musical performance in real time, such as dynamics, vibrato starting and stopping, depression of sustain pedals, and pitch bend. Since MIDI information contains only performance instructions for music playback rather than the sound data itself, MIDI data takes up relatively little space on your disk. For example, a four minute song stored in CD quality digital audio will take 40 megabytes of disk space, while the same piece saved as MIDI information might use only 70 kilobytes! For a relatively small investment in a MIDI sound module, you can get high quality sound without the high data storage overhead normally associated with CD quality audio.

MIDI synthesizers come in a variety of shapes and sizes, but basically may be seen as coming in two configurations: integrated units which contain a keyboard, performance controllers, and a sound generating system; and sound modules which are just sound generating devices and come in either rack mount or desktop models with MIDI input and output jacks for performance control.

All MIDI synthesizers will also have some form of audio output jacks as described above, and may even have input jacks so the sound from the computer can be passively mixed with the synthesizer's output allowing a single connection to your sound system for all your sound needs. Many of the newer MIDI sound modules designed for connections to computers have a direct serial interface built-in for connecting to the computer, but some still require a special device called a MIDI interface to communicate with the computer.

Figure 18 illustrates how MIDI data is routed in a MIDI synthesizer and how sound produced is outputed through the audio jacks.

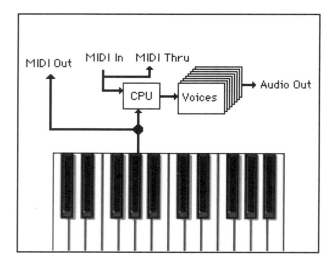

Figure 18: MIDI Control And Audio Configuration

If you have a MIDI synthesizer, you may connect it to your computer as shown in Figure 19, or according to its user's manual.

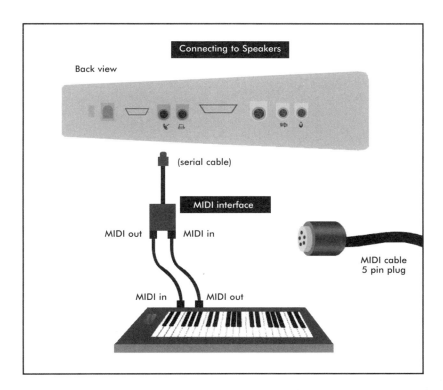

Figure 19: Connecting A MIDI Synthesizer

A real-time musical performance may be captured and stored in the computer by using a software application called a sequencer. Sequencing software stores MIDI events in the order they occur (hence the name "sequencer") for later editing and playback. Many different parts of a musical piece may be recorded individually, then played back as a complete performance. The MIDI protocol provides for sixteen discrete channels, kind of like television channels except they can all be watched (or rather, listened to) simultaneously. This allows for having up to sixteen different musical parts played at once. Today, most MIDI sound modules can play all sixteen MIDI channels at once, providing a virtual orchestra in a small box.

Sequencers store their information in a universal file format called a Standard MIDI file (often abbreviated as SMF). These MIDI sequence files contain the performance information necessary to have a MIDI synthesizer play back the music. Because the information stored is simply the performance information and not the sounds themselves (these are stored in the synthesizer), we can change the speed of playback without affecting the pitch, and we can change the pitch (transposing the key) without affecting the tempo. We can also isolate any single track within the performance either to listen to it alone (solo), or to silence (mute) it so we might perform it ourselves with the accompaniment. MIDI sequencing is the most popular use of personal computers for music. For more information specifically about MIDI, please refer to the Ultimate Beginner Tech Start Series™ book entitled MIDI BASICS (0173B) by Lee Whitmore.

Okay, now we have our computer and music workstation configured and ready to go, so let's see what we can do with our system!

Chapter Three
Practicing With A Computer

No matter what your level of playing or general musicianship, there is usually room for improvement. Life-long learning is probably one of the best attributes of a musician's lifestyle; we are always practicing, and always trying to get better. One of the great benefits of computers is that they are excellent at repetitive tasks—and they never complain about playing the same four bars over and over while you perfect the phrasing of a melodic line. They also make tireless music practice and drill partners for ear training, music theory, and composition and can provide teaching and learning materials for a variety of musical subjects as well as instrumental technique.

Let's first look at some of the available software applications for general music learning and skills development. By necessity, we will discuss some software that may be available for either Macintosh or Windows platforms only, but we will focus primarily on those tools that are available across both platforms.

Music History

There are many available multimedia-based CD-ROM products which make learning about music history enjoyable, enlightening, and entertaining. Recently a word was coined to describe these types of products: "edutainment." The first of these products was Mozart's *Magic Flute* from Warner New Media's "Audio Notes" series, and was Macintosh-only. Apple Computer released a product in 1987 called HyperCard, which was the first "multimedia authoring" software. At that time, the Macintosh was still an all-in-one form with a small black and white monitor. As a result, the early multimedia music history products were fairly low resolution in terms of graphics, but featured high quality sound from the CD.

The Magic Flute allowed you to explore Mozart's opera, its characters and themes, and learn about the music motifs and development. The following illustration shows four screens from *The Magic Flute* centered around the character Tamina.

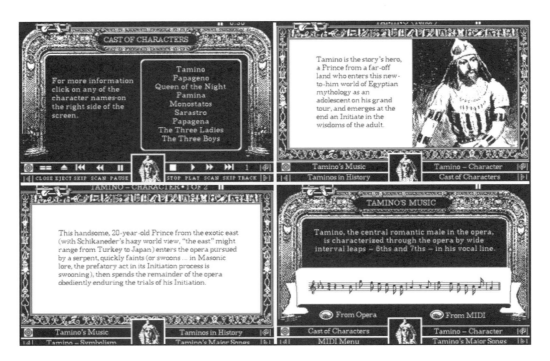

Figure 20: Warner's *Magic Flute*

Since *The Magic Flute* there have been many releases by three main software publishers: Warner, Voyager, and Microsoft. These products examine a musical work by placing the piece, its composer, and its first performances in the context of the historic period. You can listen to the audio from the CD, look at the score, view pictures of the composers and their times, and read commentary and analysis by noted musicologists and theorists. Some even include a game-like quiz to see how much you've learned about the work. Some of the newer titles feature the work of contemporary artists such as David Bowie and Peter Gabriel.

Another popular title in this category is *Microsoft Musical Instruments,* a product which allows you to explore various instruments from around the world, see pictures, hear the sounds they produce, and read a little about their history. Figures 21 and 22 show a few screens from *Microsoft Musical Instruments.*

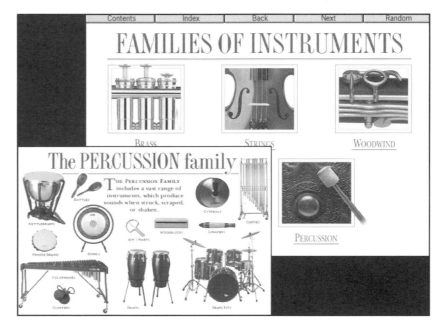

Figure 21: Instrument Families From *Microsoft Musical Instruments*

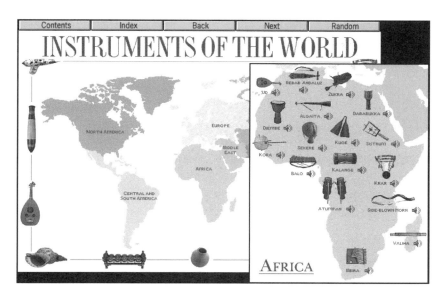

Figure 22: Instruments From Around The World

The following is a short list of some of the most popular Multimedia CD-ROM titles:

Title	Publisher
Bach and Before	Voyager CD Companion Series
Beethoven, String Quartet No. 14	Warner New Media
Beethoven, Symphony No. 9	Warner Audio Notes
Brahms, German Requiem	Warner Audio Notes
Britten, The Orchestra	Warner New Media
History of Country Music	Queue
Jazz - A Multimedia History	Compton's New Media
Microsoft Musical Instruments	Microsoft
Mozart, String Quartet in C Major	Voyager CD Companion Series
Mozart, The Magic Flute	Warner Audio Notes
Schubert, Quintet in A Major - The Trout	Voyager CD Companion Series
So You Want to be a Rock And Roll Star	Interactive Records
Strauss, Three Tone Poems	Voyager CD Companion Series
Stravinski, The Rite of Spring	Voyager CD Companion Series
Subotnick, All My Hummingbirds Have Alibis	Voyager CD Companion Series
Subotnick, Making Music	Voyager
The History of the Blues	Queue
The Resident's Freak Show	Voyager
Laurie Anderson, Puppet Motel	Voyager
Beatles, A Hard Day's Night	Voyager
David Bowie, Jump	ION
Peter Gabriel, Xplora I	Real World Media

Ear Training And Theory

Some of the greatest skills you can develop as a musician are your critical listening, aural analysis, and sight reading abilities. These skills are sharpened by the study known as Ear Training. Rather than learning to wiggle your ears, Ear Training helps you develop your inner hearing abilities; to look at music and know how it sounds; to notate or play back music by ear; and improve your improvisational skills. Theory helps in your overall understanding of music, both from a performance as well as a writing standpoint. Understanding form, harmony, rhythm and melody will improve all of your musical work. There are several excellent software programs available to help with these studies. The best known are:

Title	Publisher
Listen	Imaja Software
Inner Hearing	Musicware
Practica Musica	Ars Nova
Music Ace	Harmonic Vision
Clef Notes	Electronic Courseware Systems
Harmonic Progressions	Electronic Courseware Systems
Professor Piccolo	Opcode Systems
Music Lab	Musicware

Figure 23 shows a screen from Imaja Software's Listen. Note that Listen provides both a piano keyboard as well as a guitar fretboard for inputting responses to the ear training exercises. In the example shown, Listen will play a triad, and you will have to play the notes of the chord starting on the indicated key or fret and string. This kind of drillware is like having your own private dictation teacher who tirelessly plays examples for your practice.

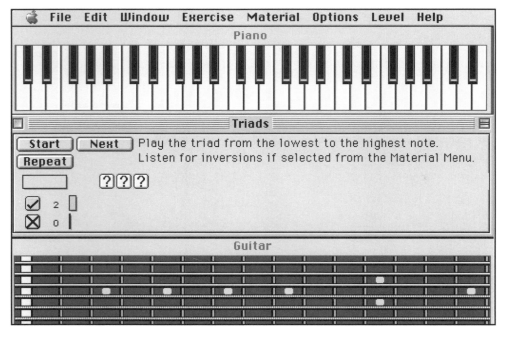

Figure 23: Imaja Software's Listen

Music Ace from Harmonic Vision is a fun program that combines beginner-level ear-training and theory into a kind of game-like environment. If you are just beginning to learn to read or just starting theory, Music Ace is a good starting point. Figure 24 shows an example from Music Ace where the program plays a note (the note actually sings—note the open mouth) and you have to play the piano key that matches the pitch sung.

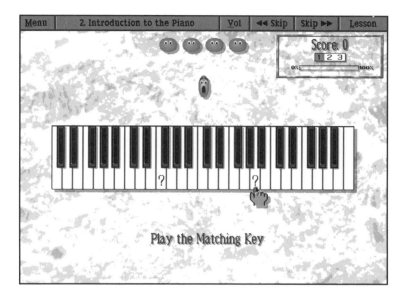

Figure 24: Music Ace

Practica Musica provides a bit more advanced drill and practice in melody, rhythm, theory and ear training exercises. Figure 25 shows a screen from Practica Musica which requires you to tap the rhythm of the displayed melody. The software will play the given example, as well as your response, so you can hear how well you did, in addition to the program's automatic grading of your work.

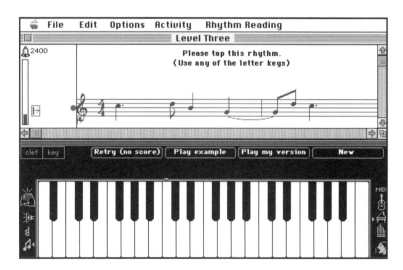

Figure 25: Practica Musica

In addition to these general music learning programs, there are some specific tools for learning to play some popular instruments as well as general purpose tools for improving one's musical performance and improvisation skills.

Instrumental Skills

While there are several excellent programs for learning to play an instrument, most focus on the two most common instruments in people's homes today—guitar and piano. The following is a short list of available titles:

Title	Publisher
Guitar 101	Lyrrus/Fender
The Jazz Guitarist	PG Music
Guitar Method	eMedia
Guitar Wizard	Baudville
The Pianist, The Modern Jazz Pianist, etc.	PG Music
The Jazz Soloist	PG Music
Jim Kelly's Guitar Workshop	Berklee Press

Let's take a look at one of these for guitar, as guitar is an acoustic instrument and we can extrapolate this example for all acoustic instruments. *Guitar 101* is from Lyrrus Incorporated, and is distributed by Fender Musical Instruments. Featuring the guitar methods of Jack Cecchini, this CD-ROM features audio, video, and graphics designed to help you learn to play guitar from an absolute beginner's perspective. The most unique aspect of this CD is that if you own the Lyrrus interactive guitar hardware called G-VOX, you can plug your guitar into the computer's serial port and everything you play will be displayed on-screen in either standard music or fretboard notation. This allows you to play along and see any mistakes you might have made.

Figure 26: *Guitar 101*

Figure 26 shows the main screen in *Guitar 101*, showing the lessons offered in Room 1. You can easily navigate to any of the other available lessons from this point. Figure 27 shows guitarist Karl Verhein demonstrating how to hold the guitar using a strap in a standing position.

Figure 27: *Guitar 101*

The many lessons on this CD-ROM take you through the basics of guitar mechanics, provide a history of Fender guitars, and show music theory from a guitarist's perspective. And if you plug in your guitar, using the optional G-VOX hardware, you can have extremely interactive guitar lessons right at home in front of your computer screen.

Performance And Improvisation

Learning music intended to be performed in an ensemble context is often difficult when practiced on a solo instrument. The computer can be a great benefit as a practicing partner at almost every level by acting as an automated accompanist. You can have a virtual rock band, jazz combo, big band, or full orchestra in your practice room by using a MIDI synthesizer along with your computer and appropriate software. Their are three basic approaches to this application:

- Using MIDI sequencing software to play back a previously recorded accompaniment piece.
- Using specialized playback software such as Coda's Vivace as an interactive accompanist.
- Using an automated rhythm section generator such as Band-in-a-Box to perform as your accompanying band.

Using A MIDI Sequencer As An Accompanist

We will discuss how you create your own MIDI sequences in Chapter Four: "Writing Music With A Computer," but there are many ways to acquire MIDI sequence files already created for use as a virtual accompanist. If you have access to the Internet, there are a variety of sites that provide MIDI sequence files freely available for download. You should be very careful when downloading these files, as many are copyrighted and your downloading and using them is a violation of applicable laws. There are some sites which provide public domain files, and some sites which provide copyrighted files for sale which appropriately compensate the composers. For more information on the Internet and downloading MIDI sequence files please refer to the book *Musicians And The Internet* (0175B) from this Ultimate Beginner Tech Start Series™.

There are many other sources for MIDI sequence files designed for accompaniment purposes available from major publishers. Warner Bros. Publications has an entire series called Performance Plus with MIDI files available and sold separately from the music itself. You load the MIDI file into the sequencer, and then play along with the printed music from the various available song folios.

Generally these files are made to work as an accompaniment for any instrument so you would load the MIDI file into your sequencing software, then choose the appropriate musical part you would be practicing. As we saw in Chapter Two, MIDI sequence files usually contain a number of musical parts, each stored in a separate track on individual MIDI channels. There are two ways to use this kind of file; you can solo the track containing the musical part you want to learn so that you can play along with it, or you can mute that part so that you can play the piece and have the accompaniment play along with your performance. Either way, you can use the sequencing software to slow the piece down to help you learn the part, then speed it back up as you gain mastery of the piece. With a MIDI sequencer, changing the tempo simply slows down the playback of the performance data, but doesn't affect the pitch. Figure 28 shows an excerpt from "Theme from Inspector Gadget" from the Performance Plus™ series (Warner Bros. Publications), with the sequence loaded into Opcode's MusicShop.

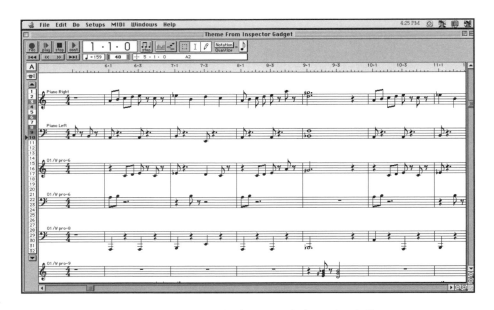

Figure 28: "Inspector Gadget" Loaded Into MusicShop

Tracks 3 and 4 are the piano part (left and right hands respectively) and other tracks are showing the accompaniment. You can of course hide the accompaniment and only see the part you are to play simply by selecting only tracks 3 and 4. If you are working on learning to improvise, you can also use the MIDI sequencer's editing controls to change the key, usually by selecting all the tracks and using a "Transpose" command. This allows you to learn to improvise over a given song or set of chord changes in every key.

Using Interactive Accompaniment Software

Recently, Coda Music Technology released a software-only version of their popular Vivace system called Vivace Practice Studio. This software allows you to use pre-recorded music files in a specialized MIDI format in an interactive accompaniment. This software is interactive in that it actually listens to your performance and follows your interpretation, providing appropriate accompaniment response: if you slow down, so will the accompaniment; if you get louder, so too does the accompaniment; skip 4 bars and the virtual orchestra skips ahead as well to keep time with you. This software is great for professional level players who want to practice their interpretation of music, not just the notes themselves.

Using An Automated Rhythm Section Generator

An automated rhythm section generator allows you to specify a given set of chord changes, choose a key, tempo, and musical style, and the software automatically creates the necessary backing tracks to accompany your performance. The most popular example of this type of software is Band-in-a-Box from PG Music. Band-in-a-Box allows you to choose from hundreds of stored songs or enter your own by typing in standard chord symbols, selecting a musical style, set the key and tempo, and click the play button to create a music-minus-one type accompaniment for your practice session. Transpose, change tempos and styles all with a simple point and click user interface. You can create your own styles using the Style Editor software, enter melodies, or record a MIDI improvisation, and even print out a lead sheet. Band-in-a-Box is a versatile value-packed software package for either Macintosh or Windows-based PCs.

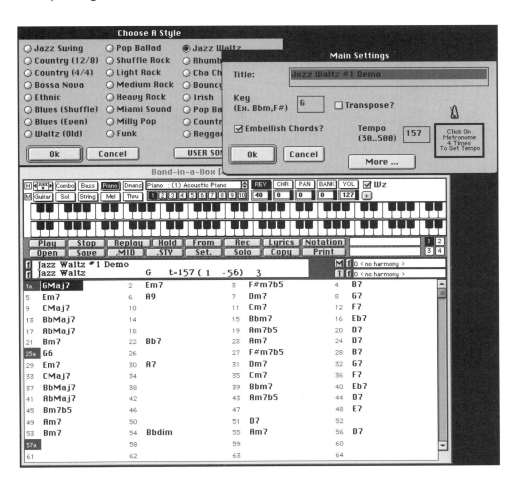

Figure 29: A Sample Screen Shot From Band-In-A-Box

Note that in the above example, two windows are shown for changing the musical style, tempo, chord voicing style, and key—allowing you to practice just about any piece of popular music in a variety of styles and tempos to meet your musical needs and tastes.

Now that we have seen how we can use the computer as a music practice partner, let's go on to see how we can create our own MIDI sequences and use music notation software to write music.

Chapter Four
Writing Music With A Computer

In my high school years, I enjoyed painting as a hobby. When I began writing music in my late teens, I was struck by the difference in the experience of writing music from that of painting, or for that matter—from any other art form. Music is unique among art forms in that it does not exist in space, only in time. With other art forms, say painting or sculpture, the work exists in space and is a tangible object. You can look at it, see it, touch it, feel it, smell or even taste it at any point during its creation or after its completion. Turn your back on it, and when you return—it's still there! Music exists only in time. You can't feel it, see it, touch it—only hear it. Stop listening even for a moment, and it may be gone forever.

If you write music in the traditional fashion with pencil and paper, when you finish your work, what you have is paper with a lot of black dots all over it. You cannot hear it—and only extremely well-trained and skilled musicians can look at the score and really hear how it sounds. In fact what you are doing is creating a set of instructions for others in how to re-create your musical idea. You never really interact with your music in the form it will finally take—as sound.

Well, the computer changes all that. Today with a computer, MIDI synthesizer, and appropriate software, you can listen to the music as you create it. You can hear it in the form it will take, and make decisions about its development by interacting with the sound in real-time. The computer actually makes the composition process more like painting or sculpting: you can make a change, listen to it and decide what to do next in the same way a painter makes a brush stroke, stands back, and decides whether to change the color slightly.

So it is no surprise that the computer has revolutionized how many composers create their music in much the same way that word processors have changed the way writers work. Revisions are simpler to make, output is more professional, and the process is more interactive and fun. Still, the computer is not writing the music any more than my word processor is writing this book—you are still in control. It is the human being that creates; the computer is simply a very powerful tool to realize the creative instinct.

There are two basic tools composers use to write music: MIDI sequencing and music notation software. There are software packages that seek to integrate notation into sequencing or vice versa, but the two applications are really fundamentally different approaches, and no integrated package works as well as either specialized program type. MIDI sequencing is about creating the musical performance itself, music notation is about creating a score and parts which tell other musicians how to perform the music. While that may not seem so fundamentally different, if we examine the difference between musical performance and notation we will better understand why these two actions are difficult to incorporate into the same software environment.

As we mentioned above, music exists only in time. In order to create a notation system for how music takes place in time, time itself needs to be quantified into discrete units. For this, early musicians came up with a system of relative time values which define when a note is played and what its duration is in relation to a specified real-time value called the tempo. Because of the need for relative time values as a quantification of time in relationship to a speed or tempo, our notation system is imperfect at describing exact durations in time. For instance, an eighth note played legato is different in duration than an eighth note played staccato, but either way, the eighth note appears the same in standard musical notation. The actual phrasing is left up to the performing musician, and will vary with every performance based on many subjective factors.

Since MIDI sequencing actually creates a performance of the music, it defies the quantification of time necessary for producing "accurate" music notation. The best software packages attempt to rectify these differences by using a quantification of time for the music notation graphic, while leaving the performance data untouched. This creates a number of problems, because music notation is an imperfect art rather than a science. If two successive notes overlap slightly to affect a very legato passage, the notation will show this overlap with tied notes, over-complicating the resulting notation beyond most musicians scope of reading ability. So depending on what your end goal, you would choose one tool or the other. Luckily, with the Standard MIDI File (SMF) format we can work in both types of applications by exporting and importing the files between software programs. This lets us create two files for the same music—a MIDI-sequenced performance of the piece and a music notation version for print output.

Music Notation

Music notation software was the first type of music software available on personal computers. The reason for this is that generally the first applications for a computer closely resemble ways we accomplished tasks before we had computers. So the first notation programs worked much like pen and paper—using the mouse and keyboard to "paint" the notation onto a score, except that now we could copy and paste, edit and revise, and print out high quality music notation. The biggest attraction for early adopters was that you could enter data into a score once, then have the computer do the drudgery of extracting and transposing all the individual instrumental parts. This alone was an overall time-saver, even if the notation entry took longer than it would with paper and pencil—and the resulting output was more professional.

After the first versions of music notation software become more widely used, people began asking for more features: why can't we enter the music by playing from a MIDI keyboard either in real or step-time. (Step-time is the process of entering each pitch, one at a time, and specifying for each what would be the duration.) Newer programs allow you to enter the pitch from the MIDI keyboard and use the alpha-numeric keyboard keypad to set the duration. This allows you to enter the music very quickly without having to be an accomplished keyboardist.

For accomplished keyboardists, the newer programs allow you to play the music into the software in real-time. Then the software guesses at the most likely rhythm and duration based on the tempo and your performance against the computer's metronome. Hardly a perfect transcription in most cases, but a fast way to input a first rough draft for later editing, adding the final polishing touches.

Regardless of the means of entry—real-time, step-time, or using the mouse and keyboard—you can enter multiple musical parts, one at a time to create an entire score. Once the score is entered, a single menu command can extract each individual part from the score, transpose it for the correct instrument, and prepare it for printout. Some programs even check to ensure that no part exceeds the normal playing range of the assigned instrument. The resulting output is high quality music notation with less time spent doing repetitive copying tasks.

The newest programs also allow you to playback your score through a MIDI synthesizer, with traditional music symbols translated into musical performance nuance. For example, adding a crescendo marking to the score actually results in the MIDI performance getting louder over the specified time. However, the performance will usually sound fairly mechanical, as all of the pitches will occur at precisely quantized time values with exact durations as specified in the notation. As we discussed earlier, notation is really a simplified way of directing other musicians in their interpretations of your score through their performance. If you really want to create a musical performance, the MIDI sequencer is the right tool.

Figures 30 and 31 show screens from two of the most popular music notation software packages.

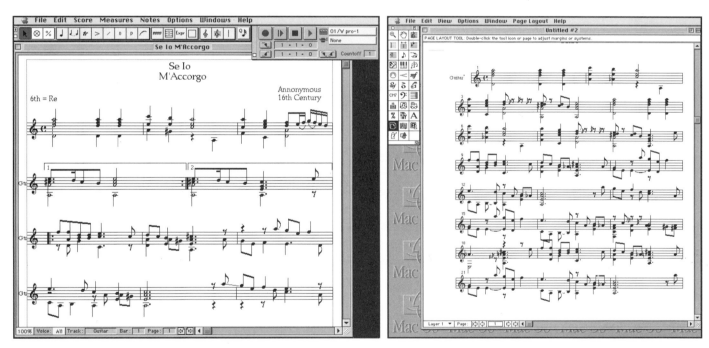

Figure 30: Screen From Opcode's Overture   Figure 31: Screen From Coda's Finale

MIDI Sequencers

We have discussed the basic concepts of MIDI sequencers in Chapters Two and Three above. Here we will delve deeper into how they work, how you can use them to create your own music, and how you can better use them for producing musical performances filled with nuance. The sequencer is probably the most popular tool for creating music at a desktop music production workstation. In most basic terms, the sequencer allows you to play music into the computer with any MIDI instrument and store it for later editing and playback.

Sequencers generally emulate the multi-track recording process: they let you play each musical part individually into a separate "track" of the sequence, usually assigning each instrument to a separate MIDI channel. Unlike the multi-track tape recorder, however, the information captured is not the sound of the instrument, but simply the performance data—which notes were played at which times. This allows us to separate totally the performance information from the resulting musical sound—so endless re-orchestrations are possible with a simple click and drag of the mouse.

As we discussed above with music notation software, the music can be played in either in real- or step-time, allowing more complex music to be entered than you might normally be able to perform. (Some people think of this as a means of cheating—but few composers can play all of the instruments he writes for, and certainly one should not be limited to write only what he can play, that would be a tremendous limitation on creativity!) Once entered, the music can be cut, copied, and pasted, transposed, repeated, inverted, played backwards (retrograde), re-orchestrated, or any compositional means applied to transform the music into exactly how you want it to sound. And with most modern software, all of these edits can be applied in real-time, while the music is playing. And if you don't like the results of your edit, a single "Undo" command returns it to its last state.

Sequencers usually allow you to view your work in a variety of useful ways. The event list view allows you to see all of the notes entered as a scrolling list showing the bar, beat and fraction (most sequencers divide each beat into 480 fractional parts, allowing for very fine timing details) of when the note was played, the pitch played, its velocity value, and its duration (again in bars, beats, and fractions). Any specific field of this data can be edited, simply by clicking in the desired location and typing in a new value; for instance you can change the loudness of the note by changing its velocity value, the pitch by changing its note number, and the timing of the note by editing its start time. Figure 32 shows a typical sequence track's event list view.

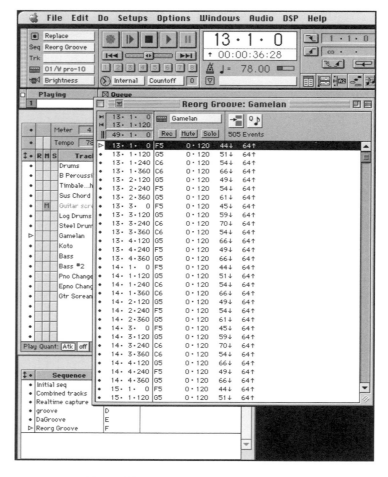

Figure 32: A MIDI Sequencer's Event List

A second useful way to work with sequencer data is the graphic view. In this view, the data is presented in a kind of "piano-roll" format where pitch is shown on the vertical axis from low to high, and time is shown on the horizontal axis, divided into measures, beats, and fractions. At the bottom of the screen is shown a bar graph depicting the velocity value for each note as a bar of varying heights. Taller bars indicate louder notes, shorter bars depict softer notes. Any of these values can be changed simply by clicking and dragging. For instance clicking on a note and dragging it up or down changes its pitch; dragging the beginning of a note forwards or backwards changes its metric placement in time; dragging the end of a note changes its duration; and dragging across the velocity graph can change the volume of a pitch or a group of pitches (allowing you to easily create dynamic changes over time). Figure 33 shows a typical graphic editing view.

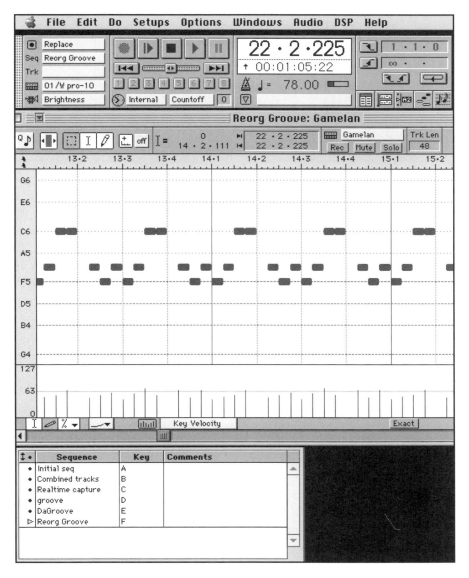

Figure 33: A MIDI Sequencer's Graphic Editing View

A third useful way to look at the data is the music notation view. This allows you to check the pitch and duration of your music in standard music notation (more or less). Most sequencers do not provide a whole palette of tools for creating professional music notation output, but provide this view simply for editing pitches in a familiar format. Once again, it is easy to move between sequencers and music notation packages using the Standard MIDI File format, using the best tool for the specific job at hand. Figure 34 shows a MIDI sequencer's music notation view.

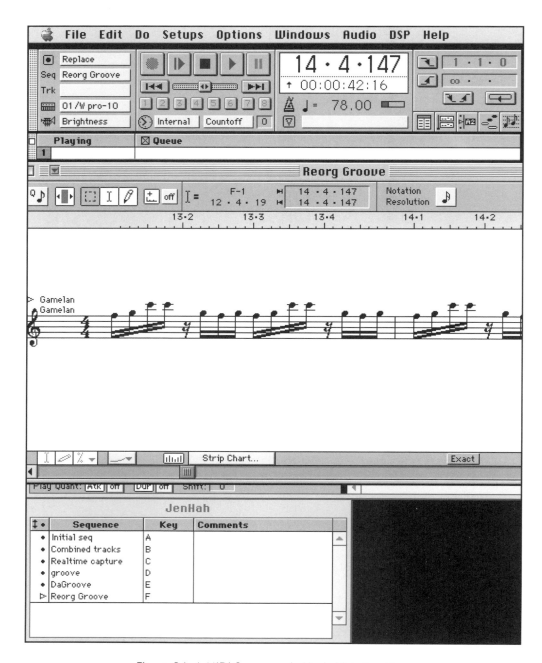

Figure 34: A MIDI Sequencer's Music Notation View

Today's sequencers sometimes have the ability to record audio directly into a track as if it were MIDI data. This allows us to combine the best of both the acoustic and electronic worlds by letting us work with MIDI and audio data in the same recording and production environment. Many sequencers also provide on-screen mixing consoles and allow you to use digital signal processing in real-time. Now you have complete control over both MIDI synthesizers and digitally recorded audio tracks for mixing, panning, equalizing, and processing sounds—all in a convenient graphic environment. Figure 35 shows the audio recording window from a popular MIDI sequencer package, including standard software-based VU meters.

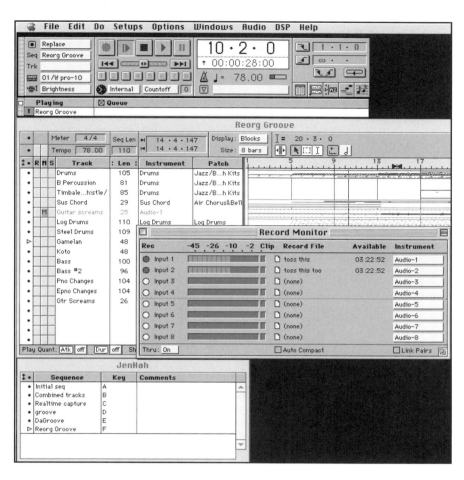

Figure 35: A MIDI Sequencer's Audio Recording Window

Figure 36 shows a mixing console in a MIDI sequencer. Some of the tracks are showing MIDI synthesizer channels, others are showing digital audio tracks complete with processing controls.

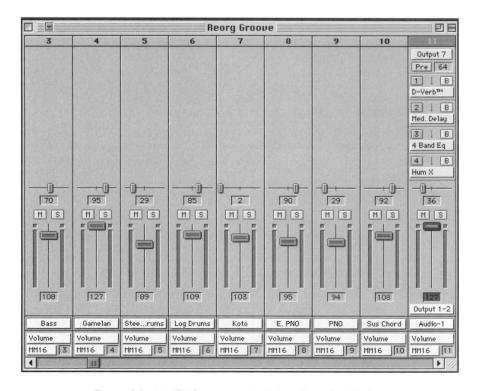

Figure 36: A MIDI Sequencer's Mixing Console Window

Obviously there is too much to cover on the topic of MIDI sequencers in a book of this size and scope, so to learn more on this subject please refer to the book *Sequencing Basics* by Don Muro (0181B), also in this Ultimate Beginner Tech Start Series™. Since we have just begun the discussion of digital audio recording in the MIDI environment, let's look at some more advanced applications for a computer in enhancing your musical productivity.

Chapter Five
Advanced Applications

As we have seen in Chapters Three and Four, there are a variety of useful applications for music-making that fall into the everyday categories of what people do without computers. In this chapter we will examine some of the popular applications for music-making which were difficult if not impossible without the use of computers.

Audio Recording And Editing

We first briefly discussed the capability for recording audio with your computer in Chapter Two. So let's discuss why we might want to record audio with your computer. Audio editing using a computer provides you with an ease and flexibility unrivaled by traditional methods. For instance, audio engineers have, for years, cut and spliced tape to affect edits in recorded audio. A simple slip of the razor blade and the music is destroyed. And it's incredibly difficult to perfectly match splice points and levels on tape to make a musically effective edit. With the computer, you can very easily experiment with edit points both visually as well as audibly. In addition, each edit is easily undone because the edits are non-destructive; that is, they are happening in temporary memory (RAM) rather than to the file itself. And with the easy-to-use tools available in most audio editing packages, you can adjust volume levels of splice points to make edits musically useful.

In many cases, audio recordings are no longer admissible in a court of law because these edits are so easy to accomplish using a computer. You may recall the famous O. J. Simpson case and the controversial "911 tapes." These tapes were not allowed as evidence because they had been "electronically enhanced" (read digitally edited) to make them more intelligible. Figure 37 shows a screen from BIAS Software's Peak, a popular audio editing software program. Note the visually distinct events; these are separate words—the file is a recording of me speaking the words "one - two - three."

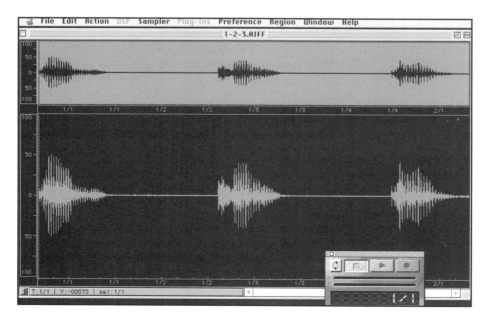

Figure 37: An Audio Editing Screen

Once the audio is stored in the computer, it can be used for many purposes: posting on a Web site (to promote your work, for example); preparing for mastering an audio CD, or for use in video production or multimedia applications. You can also use the computer as a multi-track audio recorder. There is software available that emulates a mix console, tape transport control, digital signal processing controls, and also provides visual editing tools. One such popular software package is Deck II from Macromedia. Figure 38 shows a typical screen from Deck II.

Figure 38: A Multi-track Recording Screen From Deck II

Once you have recorded and mixed your music the way you want it to sound, you can create a final stereo file and prepare to master it to a CD. Combining digital audio and MIDI sequencing allows you to write, record, and produce your music all on your desktop, and when completed, press an audio CD. Let's examine how simple it is to master your own standard Compact Disc.

Disc Mastering

Once you have created a number of sound files and stored them to disk, you can proceed to create a file used to master an audio CD. This is accomplished with a computer peripheral called a CD recorder, sometimes referred to as a CD-R drive. Today's CD-R drives provide an inexpensive means to writing CDs that can be played in any standard audio CD player, and used as a master for mass duplication by professional CD presses. These drives are available for less than $500, and usually include easy-to-use CD mastering software. Basically the process is simple:

1. First create your files and store them to disk.
2. Using the disk mastering software, create a list of songs in the desired order.
3. Specify the spacing between tracks.
4. Enter the index information.
5. Write the CD.

That's all there is to it! The next few diagrams illustrate the process using the popular CD mastering software Toast CD-ROM Pro (so-named as the process of writing a CD is often called burning—as the writer uses a laser to burn the information onto the disk—the rest of the analogy should now be apparent).

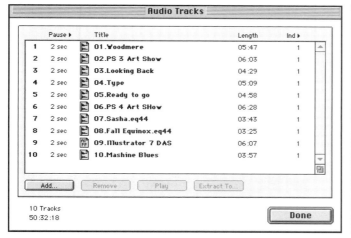

Figure 39: Creating The Song Order

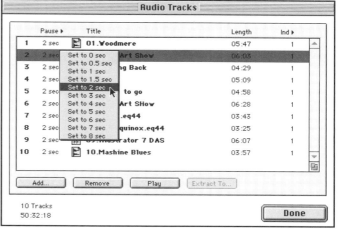

Figure 40: Specifying The Track Spacing

Figure 41: Entering The Index Information

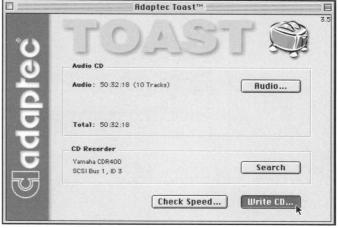

Figure 42: Writing The CD

Integrating Digital Audio And Video With MIDI Sequencers

We have already discussed how digital audio can be combined with MIDI data in a MIDI sequencing package. Let's now look at how we can also integrate digital video into our MIDI sequencing environment. There are a number of available software packages on the Macintosh that allow for seamless integration of digital audio and video into the MIDI sequencing environment. There will no doubt soon be similar offerings on the Windows platform as well, although none are available as of this writing. We'll look at Opcode's Studio Vision Pro, which we explored in Chapter Four.

Studio Vision allows you to open any QuickTime movie file directly into the program. Figure 43 shows a movie window open in a MIDI sequence.

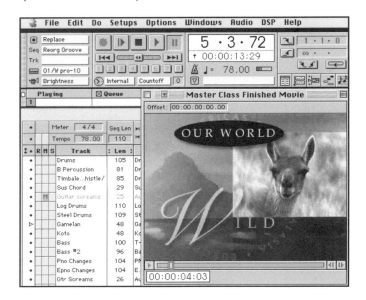

Figure 43: A Movie Window In Studio Vision Pro™

When you open the movie from the File menu, you are given the option to open only the video or to import any MIDI and/or audio files from the movie into the selected sequence. This allows you to open movies with dialog and/or sound effects tracks and add music, mix the dialog and music tracks in the console window, and then master the mixed audio back to the QuickTime movie file, playable on both Windows or Macintosh computer platforms. Figure 44 shows a QuickTime movie with audio and MIDI sequence tracks.

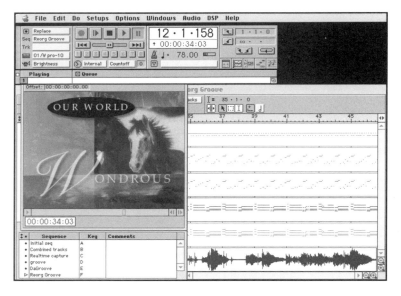

Figure 44: A Movie With MIDI And Audio Tracks

Those interested in multimedia and film scoring can further explore this concept in the book *Musicians and Multimedia* (0179B) from this Ultimate Beginner Tech Start Series™.

Sound Design

There is an entire field of work now available for musicians who can use a computer to edit and create new sounds. Sound Design is the field of work devoted to the creation of new sounds. These may be used for audio for post-production, such as sound effects for visual media, new sounds for playback through MIDI samplers, or for use on specific MIDI synthesizers. Sound design software comes in basically two formats: those which create audio sound files for playback on the computer or MIDI sampler, and those that create specialized parameter files for use in specific MIDI synthesizers, often called Patch Editors (a "patch" being the collection of instrument-specific parameters used to instruct a synthesizer to create sound).

The benefit of using a computer for sound design is that it provides you with an easy-to-use graphic interface, and far greater variety and precision in available editing tools than any stand-alone MIDI sampler or synthesizer can provide. Patch Editors give you a full screen full of data to edit with simple graphical tools instead of the usual small display provided by most of today's synthesizers. Whether creating sound files or patches for MIDI synthesizers, both means offer intuitive ways for exploration and finding new sounds, allowing you to focus on sound design concepts rather than a specific instrument's implementation of those concepts. To further illustrate this, Figures 45 and 46 show two very popular sound design software packages: Reality from Seer Systems and Galaxy Plus Editors from Opcode.

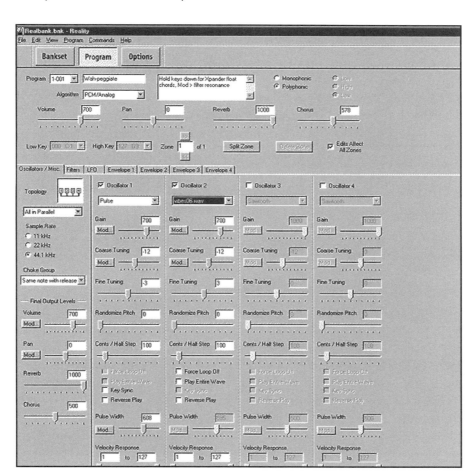

Figure 45: A Sound Design Screen From Seer Systems' Reality

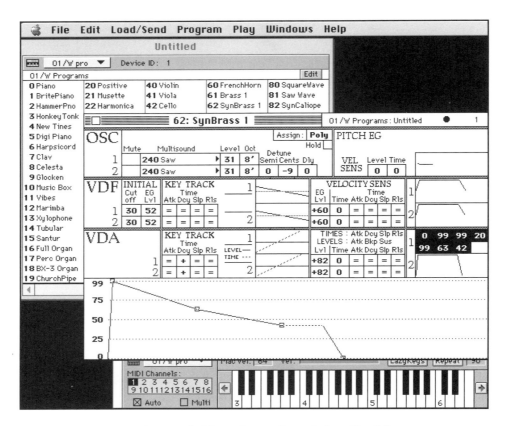

Figure 46: A Patch Editing Screen From Galaxy Plus Editors

There are excellent software packages available for both Windows and Macintosh computers. The following table shows the most popular Sound Design software available today.

Software	Publisher	Platform
Galaxy Plus Editors	Opcode	Macintosh
Unisyn	Mark of the Unicorn	Mac, Windows
Reality	Seer Systems	Windows
TurboSynth SC	Digidesign	Macintosh

In addition to offering the ability to create or edit the sounds in a MIDI synthesizer, patch editing software also provides a second function—that of organizing sounds within the synth, often called a patch librarian. The librarian component of patch editors allows you to off-load patch data (not the sounds themselves) from the synthesizer into the computer for storage, organization, and retrieval. Once the patches are in the computer, you can move them around into useful groupings; for instance, a bank of orchestral instrument sounds, a bank of jazz and popular music sounds, or a bank of sound effects. Librarian packages also allow you to quickly audition many different sounds, create a bank of sounds appropriate for your individual work, and store them on disk, so that each time you return to work on a given project, you can quickly load in your bank of sounds and continue working. The following figures show a couple of librarian screens from Opcode's Galaxy Plus Editors software.

Figure 47: A Bank Window From Opcode's Galaxy Plus Editors

Figure 48: A Library Window From Opcode's Galaxy Plus Editors

Multimedia

Multimedia is the combination of music, sound, graphics, text, and video into an interactive environment. This burgeoning field offers many new opportunities for musicians who can use the computer for adding music to these interactive projects. Common tools available allow you to add audio tracks to video and animation projects and to create interactive projects for either Macintosh or Windows platforms. The following illustration shows a screen from Macromedia Director that shows a music file (stored as digital audio) fitted to an animation track.

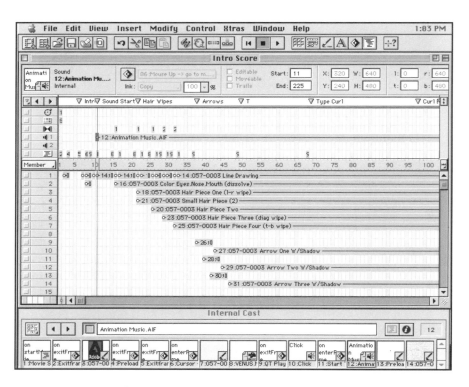

Figure 49: Music For Animation In Macromedia Director™

Figure 50 shows an Adobe Premiere project showing a finished video track with associated audio tracks for dialog (in audio track A), sound effects (tracks X1, X2, and X3) and background music (track X4).

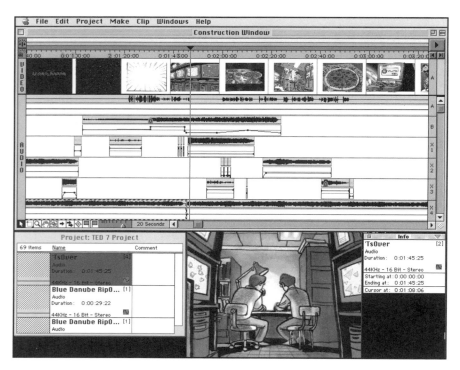

Figure 50: Music And Sound Effects In Adobe Premiere™

Again, the entire field of multimedia is too large to fully explore in a book of this size and scope. For more information, please refer to the book *Musicians and Multimedia* (0179B) from this Ultimate Beginner Tech Start Series™. Now that we have looked at a wide variety of ways for using a computer in your musical work, let's take a look at how we can use computers to help organize and manage our daily lives.

Chapter Six
Personal Productivity

In addition to all the very useful ways that we have seen for you to use your computer for music, the computer is also a powerful personal productivity tool for organizing your life, tracking contacts, promoting your work, communicating with your friends, and getting information from the Internet and World Wide Web. For the first two examples of increasing your personal productivity, we will be looking at software called a Personal Information Manager (PIM for short). One such popular PIM is ACT! from Symantec Corporation. ACT! combines a contact database with a calendar, to-do list, note pad, and word processor to help improve your ability to manage your personal and professional life. Let's start by exploring the contact management component of this software.

Contact Management

One of the most important tasks we do in our lives as musicians is keeping in touch with our friends, colleagues, business associates, and relatives. The usual means for accomplishing this with the computer is with a contact database. A database is simply a file which stores a number of records—in this case each record is a person with their contact information, much like a rolodex card. Each record will have a number of fields—blank spaces for information—which relate specifically to contact information such as name, phone number, address, e-mail address, fax number, etc. You can create a custom database for this purpose using a database management program, but more likely you will use off-the-shelf software already specifically designed for this purpose. The following figure shows an ACT! contact record screen.

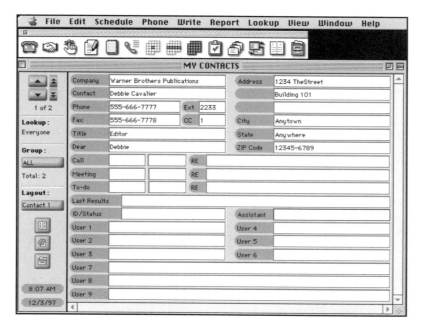

Figure 51: A Contact Record From ACT!

Note that in ACT! each record will have the same types of data, but how you view the data, or what data you choose to see may be selected from pre-stored templates or from customizable views you create yourself. These different templates are available in a pop-up menu by clicking on the Layout button on the left side of the contact record screen, as shown in Figure 52.

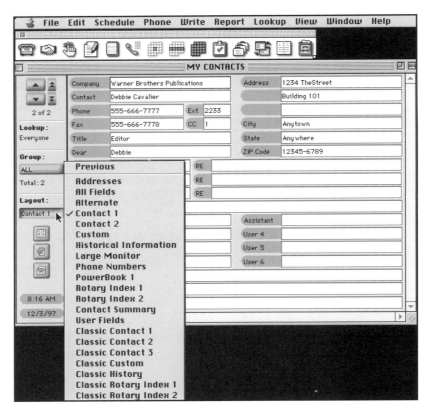

Figure 52: Selecting A Layout Template From ACT!

The following screen shows the "Phones" layout, a helpful view these days as everyone seems to have multiple phone numbers for home, work, cell phone, fax number, etc.

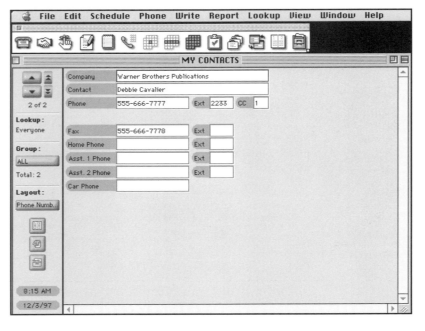

Figure 53: The ACT! Phones Layout

Once you have entered all your records and their contact information, it becomes quite easy to find a person, dial their number and track the call history. The best part of computer databases is that they are first and foremost designed to find information quickly. Figure 54 shows the various search criteria available under the Lookup menu for you to choose from to find a particular contact.

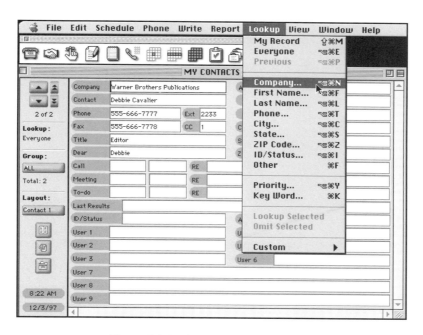

Figure 54: Lookup Options From ACT!

Once you have found the contact record, you can have the computer dial the number for you and track the call history for that person. This way, you can easily look up when you last called a manager, agent, or club owner and see the results of that call. Of course this is just one example of how you might use this feature, and you will no doubt find a host of other useful ways to keep track of your contacts. Figure 55 shows a Phone Call record from ACT! which is automatically displayed after you initiate a call from the Phone menu.

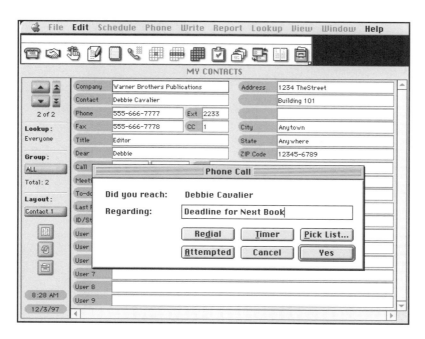

Figure 55: A Phone Call Record From ACT!

Note that if the number is busy, you can choose to redial; if there was no answer, you can log the call as "Attempted"; if the person answers, you can set the timer to track the length of the call; and when completed you can log the call by clicking on the "Yes" button (answering the question "Did you reach..."). The following screen shows the call log for a given contact.

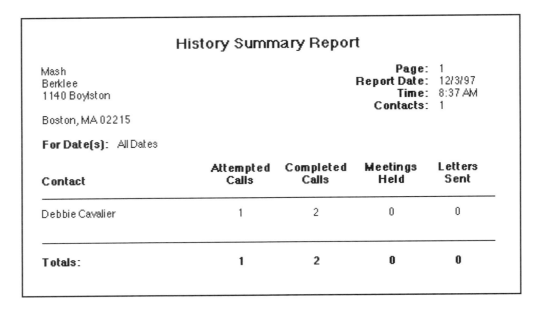

Figure 56: A Phone Call Log From ACT!

Organizing Tasks And Appointments—Calendaring

In addition to managing your contacts, ACT! allows you to manage your schedule and can integrate your contacts, calls, and meetings so that you can easily keep track of your work and personal schedule. ACT! provides day, week, and month views of your calendar and lets you easily make and track appointments, calls, and to-do tasks. You can also set alarms to remind you of appointments so you won't miss that important audition! The following screens show the week and month views of ACT!'s calendar.

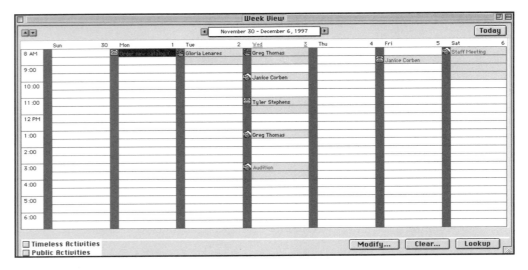

Figure 57: ACT! Calendar Week View

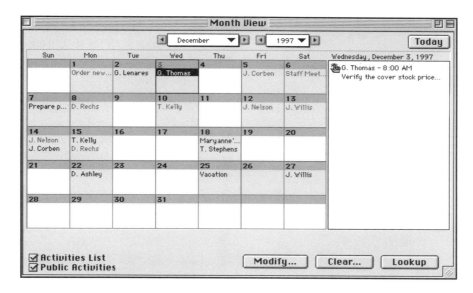

Figure 58: ACT! Calendar Month View

It is very easy to schedule an activity in ACT! Simply open the calendar by clicking on the desired view icon (day, week, or month), then click on the "Schedule..." button. In the Schedule an Activity window you can select a contact, set the date and time, the activity type (call, meeting, to-do), assign a priority and set an alarm to remind you with a specified lead time. Figure 59 shows the Schedule an Activity window in ACT!

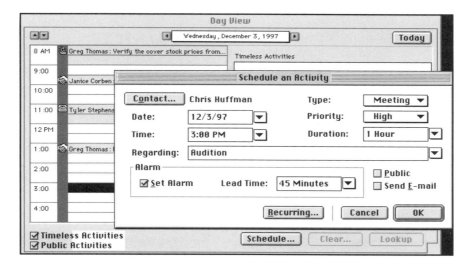

Figure 59: Scheduling An Activity In ACT!

You can also use ACT! to manage all the various tasks you need to accomplish in your daily life. To-do lists are very useful in keeping your life organized, and in monitoring your progress with various goals and projects. Figure 60 shows a calendar list with to-do tasks listed as "Timeless Activities" because often you list things to accomplish and order them by how important they are versus when you choose to schedule the particular activity.

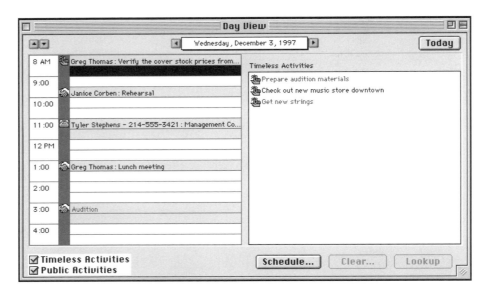

Figure 60: A To-Do List In ACT!

You can see from the prior two examples that an integrated contact manager and calendar program can be quite useful in organizing your personal and professional life. Now let's look at how you can track your income and expenses and keep your money matters organized.

Business And Finances

Tracking your income and expenses can be as easy as filling in common forms on-screen and using either a database or spreadsheet to organize and calculate figures. Let's take a look at a simple integrated office software program available for both Windows and Macintosh platforms—ClarisWorks. ClarisWorks ships with a number of templates that can be customized to fit your special needs, and which simplify tracking your income and expenses. Using simple everyday forms like deposit slips and a checkbook register, these ClarisWorks templates make it easy to enter your information. And when you need to find information, or provide it to someone else (like your accountant at tax time) ClarisWorks makes it easy with pre-built report templates. Figure 61 shows the Income and Expense Template with the variety of layouts (forms) for entering data.

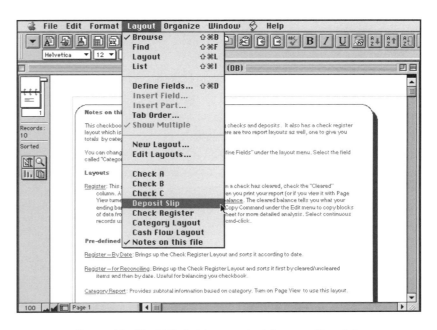

Figure 61: ClarisWorks' Income And Expense Template

Note that these templates include forms for entering deposits, writing checks, keeping a check register, and tracking cashflow. The following figures show an example of each of these templates. You will see how simple it is to use these form templates, as they so closely match their analogous real-world examples.

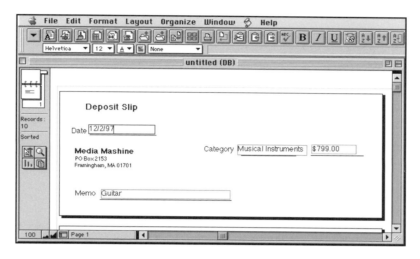

Figure 62: ClarisWorks' Deposit Form

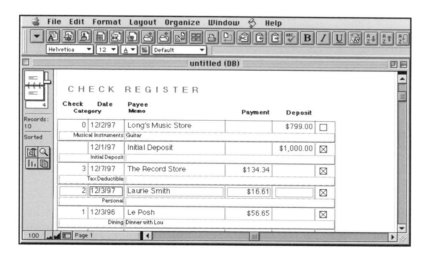

Figure 63: ClarisWorks' Check Register

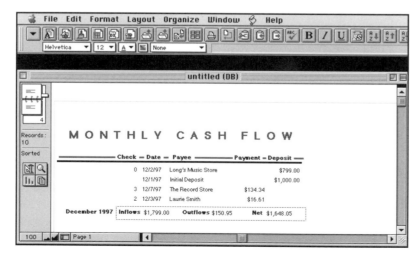

Figure 64: ClarisWorks' Cash Flow Report

In addition to these financial tracking functions, ClarisWorks is a complete office software package including word processing, drawing and painting, spreadsheet, database, communications and even simple Web page authoring. Figure 65 shows an example of using ClarisWorks' database to track your CD collection, again with a pre-built template form.

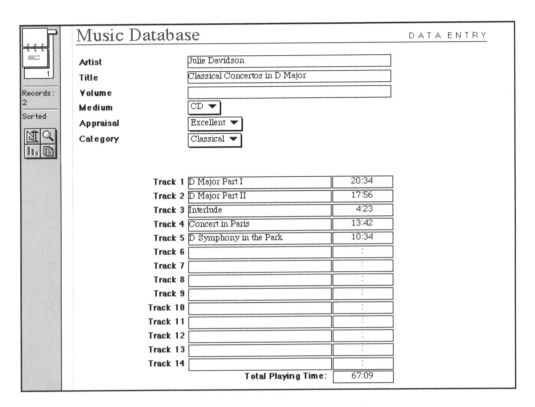

Figure 65: ClarisWorks' CD Music Database

Promotion

You can also use ClarisWorks' templates and drawing and painting tools to create promotion materials for you or your band. The "Flyers" Templates can be easily tailored to create an advertising flyer for concerts, performances or CD release parties to be publicly posted. These days, however, many musicians are using the World Wide Web as a vehicle to promote their work. The World Wide Web is a layer of the Internet—the global network of computers—which provides a graphical view of information stored as "pages" on a Web site.

Using simple authoring tools, you can create a Web site that promotes your music, allows visitors to hear audio or MIDI files, see pictures, and read news about your work. The following figures show a few screens from my personal Web site (www.mashine.com) as an example of how you can use the World Wide Web to promote your work.

Figure 66: The Media Mashine Home Page

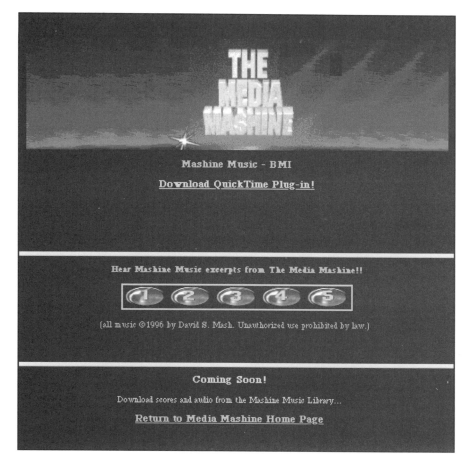

Figure 67: The Mashine Music Page

Figure 68: The Media Mashine Publications Page

Internet, E-Mail, And Web Pages

Obviously if you can promote your work to the World Wide Web, you can also use your computer to search the Internet for information about other musicians as well as sites for musical instruments, music software companies, magazines and books, as well as all the rest of services provided by the Internet. You can communicate with friends and colleagues via electronic mail, find or post information, and keep up to date with the latest news on topics of special interest to you. While the scope of this short book does not allow us to fully explore the ways you can use a computer to access the many useful resources of the "Information Superhighway," the next few screens show a few possibilities available on the Internet. For further information, please refer to the book *Musicians and the Internet* (0175B) from the Ultimate Beginner Tech Start Series™.

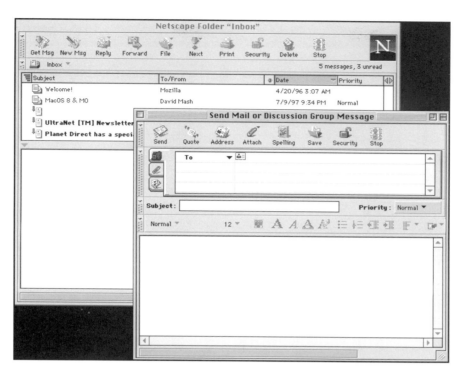

Figure 69: Internet And Electronic Mail

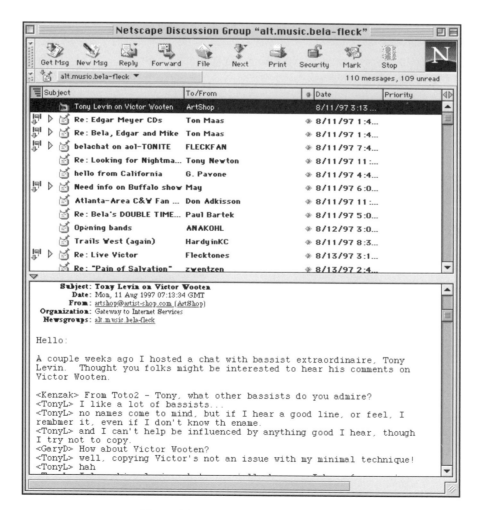

Figure 70: Internet Discussion Groups

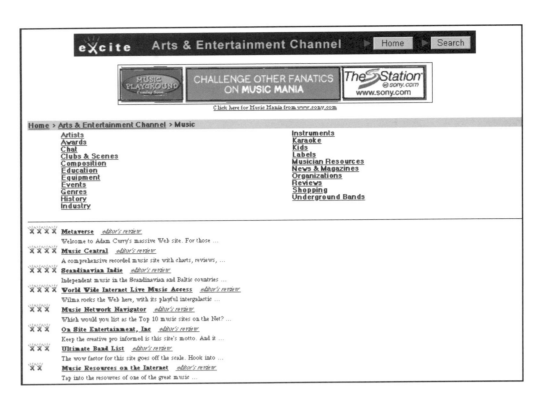

Figure 71: The Excite Arts And Entertainment Music Page

Summary

The computer can be such a useful tool for musicians, it is hard to cover every possible way to take advantage of its many benefits in any book, let alone a short introductory one such as this. You can develop your musical skills and abilities by using the computer as a practice partner, learn more about music with the many available multimedia titles, create and produce your own music with music productivity tools such as sequencers and notation programs, and promote your music via the Internet and World Wide Web.

You can organize your life with the many available personal productivity tools such as contact databases, calendars, word processors, spreadsheets and integrated office software. You can communicate with other musicians around the globe via e-mail, and stay in touch with late-breaking news on just about any topic. And best of all—it can be easy and fun! If you have a computer, start using it for music. And if you don't, start thinking about getting your hands on one as soon as possible. The computer can open many new doors for you—some you don't even know exist. Go ahead and take the plunge—a world of possibilities is available at your fingertips!

New Computer Comparison Checklist

	Computer Model 1	Computer Model 2	Computer Model 3
Brand/Model			
Processor Type			
Processor Speed			
Cache Size			
Amount of RAM			
Bus Speed			
Hard Drive Capacity			
CD-ROM Speed			
Other Storage			
Modem Speed			
Ports			
Sound Input			
Sound Output			
Monitor			
Warranty Length			
Price			

Use this convenient form when shopping for a new computer. Enter the specifications and price for each model you are considering to make a handy comparison chart. I hope this will help with the decision process.

David S. Mash

David Mash, Vice President for Information Technology at Berklee College of Music in Boston, Massachusetts, is charged with strategic planning and leadership in the successful integration of technology into all college processes. In previous roles at Berklee, David was the founding chair of the Music Synthesis Department, the first degree program in MIDI and music synthesis in the United States, now internationally recognized as the premier music technology program of its kind. He developed the Center for Technology in Music Instruction, a development center for supporting faculty's use of technology in their teaching; and helped design the Berklee Learning Center, the largest networked music learning facility in the country. The unique facilities for teaching David designed for this department have served as a model for interactive teaching environments at many major colleges and universities.

As a leading authority on music technology and education, David Mash has been featured on national and international media broadcasts such as "3-2-1-Contact," "Newton's Apple," "World Monitor," "CBS Evening News," "All Things Considered," and "Voice of America." He has also been featured on Apple Computer's video *Macintosh, Music, and MIDI—The Open Door* as well as BMG Victor's video *Macintosh Music Bible Video—Volume 1*. He has been a pioneer in music and multimedia and composed the score for the digital movie *Maria Lionza* which won the 1992 International QuickTime Movie Festival award for best documentary and is available on CD-ROM from Sumeria QuickTime: The CD 1992. He was affiliated with the Kodak Center for Creative Imaging in Camden, Maine, and taught the first music and multimedia courses offered at the center. Most recently, Apple Computer named David an Applemaster in recognition of his accomplishments in music and education.

David has collaborated on development and artistic projects with leaders in the multimedia and music industries such as Kodak, Adobe Systems, Digidesign, Opcode, and Korg and has consulted on product development for many manufacturers of music technology products. *Rolling Stone* magazine has called David "the industry's leading evangelist for the marriage of music and technology."

David is International Chair for Electronic Music for the International Association of Jazz Educators, and maintains an active schedule as speaker and presenter at national and international clinics and workshops on art, technology, and education. He has also been the recipient of grants, fellowships, and awards including a finishing grant from Apple Computer, the Arts Partnership grant for Composition/Performance, and Jazz Composition Fellowship from the Mass Council on the Arts and Humanities.

David's publications include *Musicians and Computers*, Warner Bros. Publications; *Musicians and Multimedia*, Warner Bros. Publications; *Macintosh Multimedia Machine*, Sybex; *Computers and the Music Educator*, distributed by Warner Bros. Publications; "Guide to Instructional Computing for Music Educators," National Association of Jazz Educators; "Digital Music Workstations as Creative Classroom Tools," National Association of Jazz Educators; "Future Class," *Berklee Today*; "Kurzweil 250 User's Guide," Kurzweil Music Systems; and "Technology for Teaching: Software, Synthesizers, and Sound Design," *Music Educators Journal*.